OUTDOOR ADVENTURES

FISHING

JULIE K. LUNDGREN

ROURKE PUBLISHING

Vero Beach, Florida 32964

www.rourkepublishing.com

Photo credits: Cover © Yevgen Timashov; Title Page © patrimonio; Contents Page © patrimonio; Page 4 © Bob Long, Jr. Chicago Park District, patrimonio; Page 5 © Stephen McSweeny; Page 6 © Kokhanchikov; Page 7 © Cheryl E. Davis, patrimonio; Page 8 © Jody Dingle; Page 9 © Kateryna Dyellalova, Jakub Cejpek, Mark Herreid, Fedor Kondratenko; Page 10 © Bob Long, Jr. Chicago Park District; Page 11 © Bob Long, Jr. Chicago Park District, patrimonio; Page 12 © Bob Long, Jr. Chicago Park District; Page 13 © Katrina Brown; Page 14 © Cathleen Clapper, patrimonio; Page 15 © Jody Dingle; Page 16 © Jens Stolt; Page 17 © Serge Lamere; Page 18 © Gina Smith; Page 19 © Peter Zachar; Page 20 © Lepas, patrimonio; Page 21 © Steve Brigman; Page 22 © Yevgen Timashov

Editor: Meg Greve

Cover and page design by Nicola Stratford, Blue Door Publishing

Library of Congress Cataloging-in-Publication Data

Lundgren, Julie K.
  Fishing / Julie K. Lundgren.
      p. cm. -- (Outdoor adventures)
  Includes index.
  ISBN 978-1-60694-369-4
  1. Fishing--Juvenile literature. 1. Title.
  SH445.L86 2010
  799.1--dc22

                              2009007141

Printed in the USA

www.rourkepublishing.com - rourke@rourkepublishing.com
Post Office Box 643328 Vero Beach, Florida 32964

CONTENTS

WISHING FOR FISHING

Throughout history, people have caught fish for food. Today, the sport of fishing attracts new fans every year. People who fish, called anglers, enjoy the challenge, fun, and excitement of the fishing tradition as well as tasty meals.

Depending on the body of water and the fish in it, people use different fishing methods. **Trout** anglers often use a technique called **fly-fishing**. Though ocean fishing offers a chance for huge fish, many people learn to fish on freshwater lakes and rivers.

Depending on the lake you choose, you may catch a fish your first time out.

Not even winter can stop people from fishing. Northern anglers cut holes in lake ice and drop a line. This should only be done with an experienced adult.

rod

line

reel

TOOLS OF THE TRADE

Gear up for a great day! A rod and reel gets the bait out to the fish. The rod guides and **casts** the fishing line. Rods come in different lengths. They may be stiff or flexible. The reel attaches to the rod near the rod handle. The reel stores the line and controls it as it goes in and out.

Anglers use different kinds of reels. Beginners often use spin casting reels. Spin casting reels have a handle on the side that cranks in the line.

Fishing line comes in several colors. Choose a color that makes the line look invisible underwater.

TRY IT!

To cast with a spin casting reel:

1. Press and hold the button and bring the rod back.

2. Release the button as you whip the rod forward, pointing the tip of the rod in the direction you want to cast. Make sure no one is standing behind or in front of you.

3. Turn the handle a little until you hear the reel click. That stops the further release of line.

An angler's tackle box holds small tools like needle-nose pliers and scissors alongside **bobbers**, hooks, **sinkers**, line, and **lures**. Start small and add to your collection over time, as you learn what gets results. Keep your tackle box neat and organized so you can find what you need quickly.

needle-nose pliers

bobber

sinker

lure

line

swivel

leader

Anglers often attach their hooks and lures to a short piece of line or wire called a leader. The leader clips to a swivel tied to the end of the line. Swivels turn freely so the line does not get twisted. They also allow anglers to easily remove the leader to exchange it for a different leader and lure.

This successful angler shows off her catch, holding the leader just below the swivel.

lure

YOUR FISHING MISSION: SAFETY

Life vests come in many sizes to fit any angler. Everyone should buckle one on, even if you know how to swim.

Safety is the most important part of fishing, not which bait to use or catching the biggest fish. Learn to swim. Attend a water safety course. Wear sunscreen, sunglasses, and a hat. Hats and sunglasses also protect you from stray hooks. Always wear a life vest when you are on a boat.

Listen to a weather report before heading out. Bring along food, water, a first aid kit, rain gear, and extra clothes in case temperatures drop or you get wet. If rain and wind start kicking up waves or you see a storm coming, get off the water.

Invite a friend fishing. You can watch out for each other.

TOP TIP

Take care while casting so you avoid hooking overhead power lines, trees, or your fishing buddy.

HERE, FISHY, FISHY, FISHY

Fishing might sound easy. Offer passing fish some tasty bait and when one bites, just reel it in. The challenge of fishing, however, is knowing what bait will work, where and when to use it, and how to move it so it looks real.

When your bobber starts to dance, a fish is nibbling. When the fish pulls it under, give the rod an upward jerk to set the hook firmly in the fish's mouth and then reel it in.

Fishing with a bobber on your line keeps the bait from sinking to the bottom of the lake.

Crappies like to eat small fish and freshwater insects. They travel in groups called schools.

For fishing success, learn as much as you can about fish and their habits. Freshwater **panfish**, like sunfish, **crappies**, and bluegill, often hang around docks, weed beds, and other areas protected from waves and bigger fish. Cast from shore or a dock.

16

To bait your hook with a squirmy earthworm, firmly pick one up and press the tip of the hook through once. Wrap the worm around the hook and press the tip through the worm again. Leave the wiggly ends of the worm free to help attract a hungry fish.

Other tasty morsels tempt fish. Walleye or bass waiting in a field of underwater grasses and weeds sometimes bite on leeches or minnows. Attach leeches to your hook using needle-nose pliers if you do not like how they feel when you touch them.

Northern pikes put up a fight with their large size and super strength. Get the net and the camera!

Fish that feed on other fish may strike on lures that look like a swimming fish. Anglers cast and reel in the lure again and again. As the lure pulls through the water, it moves from side to side or up and down. Twitching the rod occasionally while reeling makes the lure dart and dive like a real fish.

After fishing, **clean** your catch. Remove the guts, scales, fins, and head, and then, if you wish, **fillet** slices of meat off the bones. Fillet knives have long, thin, sharp blades. Ask an adult to help.

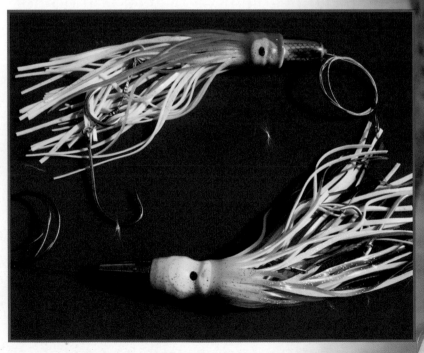

These lures can be used for deep sea fishing. They come in different weights for fishing at different depths.

Large lures may have more than one set of hooks.

19

FISHING FUTURE

Responsible anglers buy the proper licenses. They follow laws about the size, kind, and number of **keepers** allowed. Many anglers catch and release fish so they can catch them again another day. These anglers often use hooks without **barbs**. Barbless hooks can be removed more easily from fish and do not cause as much damage.

Pick up trash, hooks, and cut line. Stop the spread of **nonnative** plants and animals by cleaning your boat before going to another lake. Save leftover live bait for another trip or throw it in the garbage. It may seem cruel, but dumping it into the water can harm the animals that already live there. The new animals compete for their food and shelter.

Bait dumping has caused the spread of the rusty crayfish from its home in Illinois, Ohio, and Kentucky to many other U.S. states.

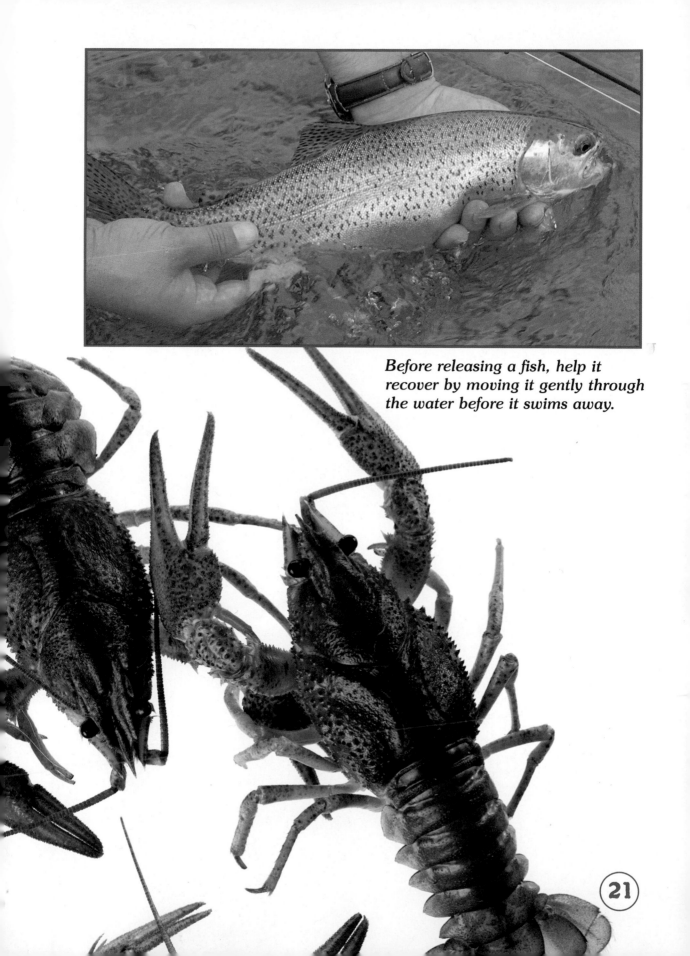

Before releasing a fish, help it recover by moving it gently through the water before it swims away.

Many fishing groups sponsor kid-friendly special events complete with food, prizes, and expert advice. Anglers love to share their sport. They hope that the thrill of a first catch will start new anglers off on a lifetime of fishy fun.

Glossary

barbs (BARBZ): sharp projections on fish hooks that make hook removal more difficult

bobbers (BAH-berz): floats, often made of cork, wood, or colored plastic, that attach to a fishing line to keep live bait hanging at a set water depth

casts (KASTS): throws a baited line into the water in a controlled way using a fishing rod

clean (KLEEN): prepare a fish for cooking by removing parts that cannot be eaten

crappies (KRAH-peez): kinds of freshwater panfish related to sunfish, like the black crappie and the white crappie

fillet (fuh-LAY): slice the flesh away from the bones using a sharp knife

fly-fishing (FLY-fish-ing): a way of fishing that uses a rod and reel to cast man-made baits, or flies, so they briefly touch on the water's surface, like an insect landing

keepers (KEE-perz): fish big enough to keep when caught

lures (LOORZ): man-made baits that look and move like the natural foods that fish eat, like minnows and other small fish

nonnative (nahn-NAY-tihv): from another place, not natural to the area

panfish (PAN-fish): flat, round fish that eat vegetation and small fish, named because they fit well in an angler's frying pan

sinkers (SINK-erz): small metal weights that attach to a line to keep the bait from floating

trout (TROWT): a kind of freshwater fish that lives in cold waters, especially mountain streams

Index

Websites

www.americaoutdoors.com/fishing/fishingfun/index.html

www.dnr.state.mn.us/fishing/index.htmlwww.fws.gov/

www.nebworks.com/kids/kids.html

www.ncfisheries.net/kids/

www.recreation.gov

About The Author

Julie K. Lundgren grew up near Lake Superior where she reveled in mucking about in the woods, picking berries, and expanding her rock collection. Her interest in nature led her to a degree in biology. She currently lives in Minnesota with her husband and two sons.